★ DISCOVERING ★
TITANIC

SEARCHING FOR THE STORIES
BEHIND THE SHIPWRECK

BEN HUBBARD

CARLTON KIDS

THIS IS A CARLTON BOOK

Published in 2018 by Carlton Books Limited, an imprint of the
Carlton Publishing Group, 20 Mortimer Street, London W1T 3JW

Text and design copyright © Carlton Books Limited 2018

Author: Ben Hubbard

Design, illustration and editing: Dynamo Limited

A catalogue record for this book is available from the British Library.

ISBN: 978-1-78312-412-1

Printed in China

10 9 8 7 6 5 4 3 2 1

CONTENTS

TALE OF TITANIC

CHAPTER 1

1912

1985

THE LASTING LEGEND

ON APRIL 10, 1912, THE MOST FAMOUS SHIP ON THE PLANET set sail from Southampton, England. It was the maiden voyage of *Titanic*, the largest ship in the world. *Titanic*, however, was doomed. She would hit an iceberg and sink four days later.

> " *I cannot imagine any condition which would cause a ship to founder. I cannot conceive of any vital disaster happening to this vessel. Modern ship building has gone beyond that.* "
>
> ★ **EDWARD SMITH**
> **TITANIC CAPTAIN**

Foremast

Crow's nest

Bridge

Lifeboats

Compass navigating platform

Crew quarters

TITANIC TICKET

Titanic was one of many passenger liners built in the early 20th century to transport European immigrants to a new life in America. Most people moving to the United States travelled in third class, but by offering luxurious second- and first-class accommodation, *Titanic* made herself the most desirable liner in the world. As such, *Titanic's* maiden voyage from Southampton to New York was a big event and many wealthy people bought a ticket.

Over 700 passengers bought a third-class ticket for *Titanic*. The cost was around £7 (about £750 today), one way.

A first-class ticket for *Titanic* cost between £30 for a single berth and £870 for a parlour suite.

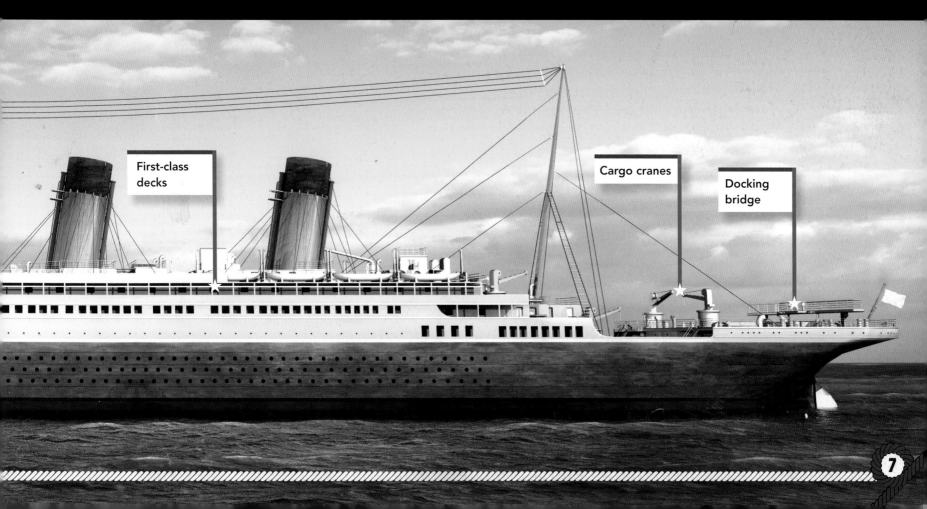

First-class decks

Cargo cranes

Docking bridge

THE UNSINKABLE SHIP

TITANIC WAS CONSTRUCTED during a time of great ship-building. She was designed to stay afloat even if flooded. The newspapers called her 'virtually unsinkable'.

> *If you had seen or known the process of extra work that went into the ship, you'd say it was impossible to sink her.*
>
> ★ **JIM THOMPSON**
> *TITANIC* WORKER

MIGHTY ENGINEERING

Titanic's hull was made of a central frame covered with a skin of long, steel plates. The plates were bolted into place using over three million iron and steel rivets. The middle of *Titanic's* hull was divided into 16 watertight compartments by special partitioning walls called bulkheads. According to her designers, even if four of *Titanic's* compartments were flooded, she would still stay afloat.

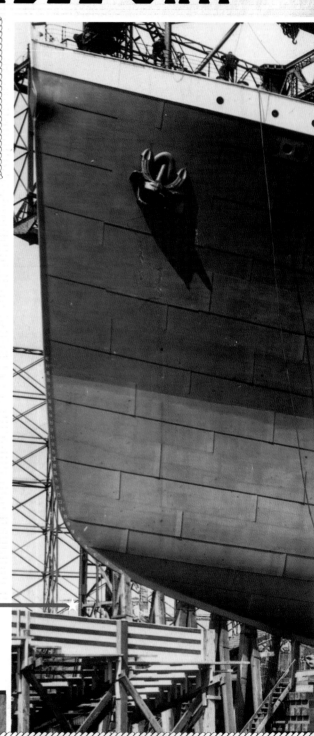

Recovered from the ocean bottom, this section of *Titanic's* hull shows the vast number of steel and iron rivets used in its construction.

Over 15,000 workers built *Titanic* in a special ship-building dock called a slipway. The slipway was then greased to ease *Titanic* into the water.

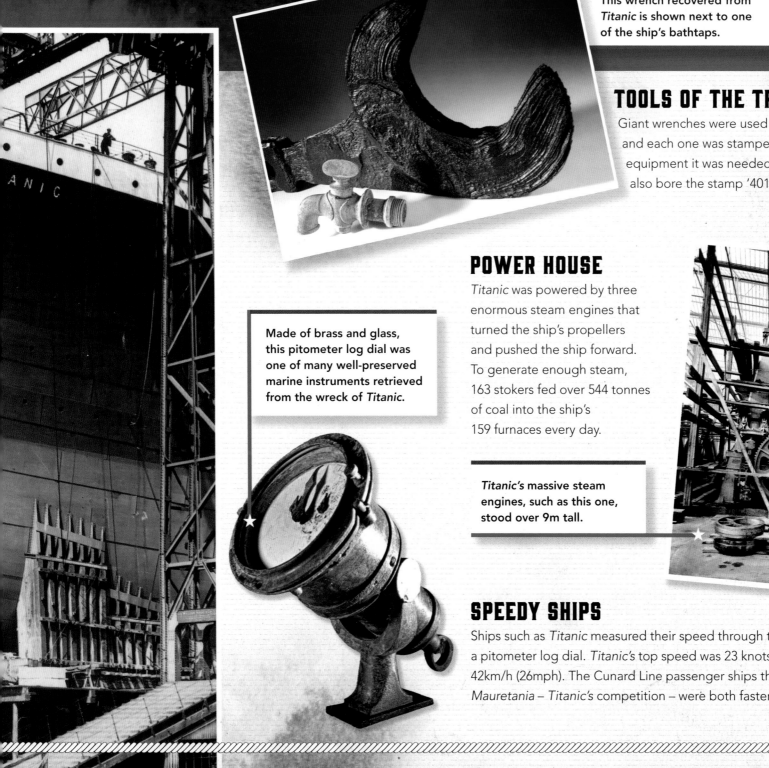

This wrench recovered from *Titanic* is shown next to one of the ship's bathtaps.

TOOLS OF THE TRADE

Giant wrenches were used to service *Titanic* and each one was stamped with the piece of equipment it was needed for. *Titanic*'s tools also bore the stamp '401': its shipyard number.

POWER HOUSE

Titanic was powered by three enormous steam engines that turned the ship's propellers and pushed the ship forward. To generate enough steam, 163 stokers fed over 544 tonnes of coal into the ship's 159 furnaces every day.

Made of brass and glass, this pitometer log dial was one of many well-preserved marine instruments retrieved from the wreck of *Titanic*.

Titanic's massive steam engines, such as this one, stood over 9m tall.

SPEEDY SHIPS

Ships such as *Titanic* measured their speed through the water using a pitometer log dial. *Titanic*'s top speed was 23 knots, which is just over 42km/h (26mph). The Cunard Line passenger ships the *Lusitania* and *Mauretania* – *Titanic*'s competition – were both faster.

A FLOATING WONDER

> *My pretty little cabin with its electric heater and pink curtains delighted me, its beautiful lace quilt, and pink cushions, and photographs all round it all looked so homey.*
>
> ★ **LADY DUFF GORDON**
> **FIRST-CLASS PASSENGER**

TITANIC PRIDED ITSELF ON BEING THE MOST LUXURIOUS and technologically advanced ship in the world. Its ultra-modern features included electric lights, elevators, telephones and a wireless radio system. *Titanic* also offered passengers comforts such as a gym, a swimming pool and exotic Turkish baths.

Even the cargo areas were divided according to class.

The grand staircase was the centrepoint of the first-class area.

The most expensive first-class suite had its own enclosed deck.

★ BATH TIME ★

The Turkish baths contained a steam room, hot and cool rooms, a shampooing room and loungers heated by electric lamps. Five stewards were on hand to help.

BRIGHT LIGHTS

The recent development of electric lighting was used to maximum effect throughout *Titanic*. This chandelier designed in the style of French King Louis XVI contained electric bulbs. Its metal became twisted and crumpled as the ship went down.

Second class included bars, saloons, a barber shop and cabins superior to first class on other ships.

The engines used steam to power *Titanic* through the ocean.

No. 251
WHITE STAR LINE.
R.M.S. "TITANIC."
This ticket entitles bearer to use of Turkish or Electric Bath on one occasion.
Paid 4/- or 1 Dollar.

No. 251
WHITE STAR LINE.
R.M.S. "TITANIC."
This ticket entitles bearer to use of Turkish or Electric Bath on one occasion.
Paid 4/- or 1 Dollar.

Only first-class passengers could buy a ticket to the Turkish baths.

Third-class accommodation for women and families was at the back of the boat.

A MATTER OF CLASS

TITANIC WAS STRICTLY DIVIDED INTO DIFFERENT CLASSES. Those in third class were not allowed to venture into the luxurious areas enjoyed by first class. However, *Titanic* aimed to attract passengers from all classes by offering them a better level of service than competing liners.

> *Tonight, after dinner, we first listened to the band, and then went up by lift to the top deck. It was glorious.*
>
> ★ **KATE BUSS**
> **FIRST-CLASS PASSENGER**

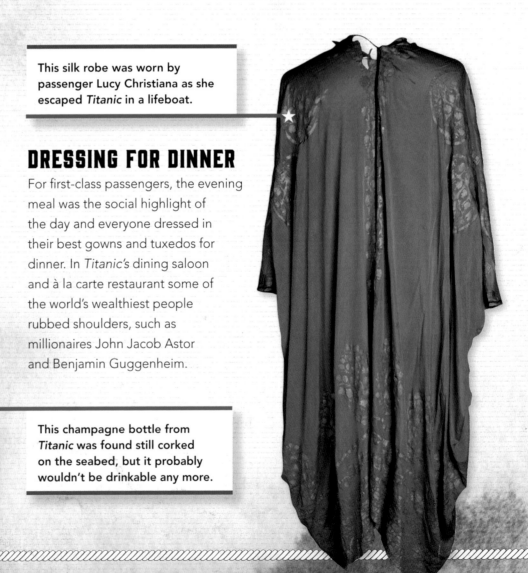

This silk robe was worn by passenger Lucy Christiana as she escaped *Titanic* in a lifeboat.

DRESSING FOR DINNER

For first-class passengers, the evening meal was the social highlight of the day and everyone dressed in their best gowns and tuxedos for dinner. In *Titanic's* dining saloon and à la carte restaurant some of the world's wealthiest people rubbed shoulders, such as millionaires John Jacob Astor and Benjamin Guggenheim.

HIT THE BOTTLE

Titanic carried over 1,000 bottles of wine and offered ten different types of champagne. However, the ship was not christened in the traditional way by smashing a champagne bottle on its hull. Many said this was a bad omen.

This champagne bottle from *Titanic* was found still corked on the seabed, but it probably wouldn't be drinkable any more.

Many of the plates recovered from *Titanic* were found neatly stacked on the sea floor, as they had been in their cupboards.

This shows the strict class structure on *Titanic*. The small teacup with gold detail is from first class, the blue and white plate is from second class and the white teacup is from third class.

OLD CHINA

Titanic carried over 57,600 items of crockery, including teacups, saucers, egg cups, plates and bowls. Each class had its own, distinctive style of china. First class ate from the finest bone china, hand-painted with turquoise and gold patterns. Third class were served from simple white plates bearing the emblem of White Star, the company that owned *Titanic*.

★ FINE DINING ★

All passengers on *Titanic* enjoyed sit-down meals at tables dressed with white linen and served by waiters. But those in first class were treated to a seven-course dinner.

66 *They said the Titanic has enough food to feed a small town. On the menu, they had things like curried chicken and rice, baked haddock with sharp sauce, spring lamb with mint sauce and roast turkey with cranberry sauce as their main dishes.* 99

★ **MADELEINE VIOLET MELLINGER**
13-YEAR-OLD SECOND-CLASS PASSENGER

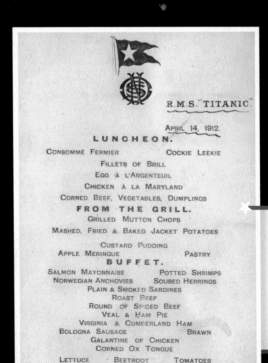

R.M.S. "TITANIC"

APRIL 14, 1912.

LUNCHEON.

CONSOMMÉ FERMIER   COCKIE LEEKIE
FILLETS OF BRILL
EGG À L'ARGENTEUIL
CHICKEN À LA MARYLAND
CORNED BEEF, VEGETABLES, DUMPLINGS
FROM THE GRILL.
GRILLED MUTTON CHOPS
MASHED, FRIED & BAKED JACKET POTATOES

CUSTARD PUDDING
APPLE MERINGUE   PASTRY
BUFFET.
SALMON MAYONNAISE   POTTED SHRIMPS
NORWEGIAN ANCHOVIES   SOUSED HERRINGS
PLAIN & SMOKED SARDINES
ROAST BEEF
ROUND OF SPICED BEEF
VEAL & HAM PIE
VIRGINIA & CUMBERLAND HAM
BOLOGNA SAUSAGE   BRAWN
GALANTINE OF CHICKEN
CORNED OX TONGUE
LETTUCE   BEETROOT   TOMATOES
CHEESE.
CHESHIRE, STILTON, GORGONZOLA, EDAM,
CAMEMBERT, ROQUEFORT, ST. IVEL.
CHEDDAR

Iced draught Munich Lager Beer 3d. & 6d. a Tankard.

Highlights from this first-class menu included potted shrimp and custard pudding. It would be the last lunch for many.

FIXTURES & FITTINGS

TITANIC WAS DECKED OUT IN THE FINEST FIXTURES AND FITTINGS to make it the most luxurious liner afloat. Everything was brand new and specially built for the ship: from its ornately carved wooden staircases to its brass door handles and stained-glass windows.

> 66 *This boat is giant in size and fitted up like a palacial hotel. The food and music is excellent… So far we have had very good weather. If all goes well we will arrive in New York on Wednesday A.M.* 99
>
> ★ **ALEXANDER OSKAR HOLVERSON**
> **FIRST-CLASS PASSENGER**

When Robert Ballard took the first images of *Titanic* in 1985, he revealed the ship's grand staircase had been smashed away as it sank. However, the cherub statue remained.

ONE STEP IN TIME

Situated at the centre of first class, the grand staircase was considered *Titanic's* main artistic feature. Illuminated by a glass dome in its ceiling that let in natural light, the staircase featured wood and wrought-iron banisters, carved oak panelling and sweeping steps laid with white tiles. At the bottom, the staircase was adorned with a bronze statue of a cherub holding a crystal lamp.

A robotic arm from a deep-sea submarine investigating the *Titanic* retrieves a stained-glass window from the wreck.

BROUGHT TO LIGHT

Stained-glass windows featured prominently in *Titanic's* first-class areas, such as its smoking room and lounge. The windows were often created in an arch shape and placed over the ship's small, round portholes. This was to make passengers feel like they were not at sea. At night the windows were illuminated with electric lights on the outside, to give the impression of daylight inside.

★ WHO'S ON BOARD ★ TITANIC?

1,317 passengers
OVER 880 crew
69 restaurant staff
8 orchestra members
6 lookouts
5 mail clerks
2 window cleaners

HANDLE WITH CARE

Many metal fixtures from *Titanic*, such as door handles, light fittings and bath taps were found in fairly well-preserved condition after 73 years on the ocean floor. Running water was a luxury not all third-class passengers would have enjoyed at home, but it was available in their cabins on *Titanic*. However, the 710 third-class passengers only had two baths to share. First-class suites had baths, showers and toilets, but the captain's bathroom was even more elaborate. His bathtub had taps delivering both hot and cold freshwater and seawater.

This chrome-plated door handle recovered from *Titanic* once opened the door to the cool room in the Turkish baths.

6:00 AM
APRIL 13
1912

FOR THE FIRST FEW DAYS OF *TITANIC'S* VOYAGE, passengers felt like they were on a relaxing holiday. There was little to do but stroll around the decks, read, play games and enjoy the ship's food. Then, as the ship entered 'Iceberg Alley', everything changed.

> *My mother had a premonition and she never went to bed in that ship at night at all. She sat up for three nights so she slept during the day.*
>
> ★ **EVA HART**
> **TITANIC SURVIVOR**

ENTERING THE WATER

The launch of *Titanic* from its slipway into the River Lagan was a big event for the people of Belfast, Ireland. Once launched, tugboats pulled *Titanic* to a fitting-out basin to have its machinery installed and rooms constructed.

No. 193

No. 193

No. 193

"TITANIC" Launch.

Launch
OF
White Star Royal Mail Triple-Screw Steamer
"TITANIC"
At BELFAST,
Wednesday, 31st May, 1911, at 12·15 p.m.

To be retained for admittance to Stand.

TO BE PRESENTED AT GATE.

Those with a ticket could watch *Titanic's* launch from inside the Belfast docks.

An onboard gym with exercise machines was one of the popular highlights of *Titanic's* first class accommodation.

ICY DANGER

Icebergs were common in the North Atlantic stretch of water known as Iceberg Alley. This photo, taken from a ship on April 15, 1912, was claimed to be of the iceberg that struck *Titanic*.

A handful of *Titanic's* deckchairs were recovered and later auctioned. One sold in 2015 for £100,000.

Icebergs in Iceberg Alley commonly broke away from glaciers in Greenland.

DECKCHAIRS

Extra space had been made on the first class top deck by reducing the number of lifeboats in the original plans. This provided more room to stroll and sit in deckchairs, but there were not enough lifeboats for all the passengers. Instead when *Titanic* sank, many tried to stay afloat on objects such as deckchairs.

★ ROYAL MAIL STEAMER *TITANIC* ★

RMS *Titanic* was a British Royal Mail ship that employed five clerks. All of them drowned trying to protect the mail as *Titanic* sank.

> *I urged them to leave their work. They shook their heads and continued at their work. It might have been an inrush of water later that cut off their escape, or it may have been the explosion. I saw them no more.*

★ **ALBERT THEISSINGER**
STEWARD DESCRIBES HOW *TITANIC'S* CLERKS TRIED TO SAVE THE MAIL

White Star Line R. M. S. *Titanic*

POST CARD

THIS SPACE MAY BE USED FOR CORRESPONDENCE

ADDRESS TO BE WRITTEN HERE

Mrs J. W. Gill
3 Griffin Rd
Clevedon
Nr Bristol

Passenger John William Gill mailed this postcard to his wife before *Titanic* sailed. He did not survive.

THE SINKING ★ SHIP

DEADLY STRIKE

11:40 PM
APRIL 14
1912

THE NIGHT OF APRIL 14 was clear, calm and bitterly cold as *Titanic* steamed through the freezing Atlantic waters. At 11:40pm the two lookouts in the crow's nest saw a large object only 457m in front of the ship. They quickly rang the bell and called the bridge with the emergency news: iceberg dead ahead!

EVASIVE MANOEUVRE

The officer on the bridge immediately ordered *Titanic* to be turned and the engines reversed. His plan was to slow the ship and steer it out of harm's way at the same time. But *Titanic* was too big and moving too fast to avoid a collision. As the ship turned, its side scraped along the iceberg, leaving tears in its hull. Freezing seawater started gushing into the ship's bulkheads.

THE SHIP IS SINKING

Titanic was constructed with 16 bulkheads that separated its hull into compartments. The theory was that *Titanic* could stay afloat if up to four were flooded. However, there were gaps between the bulkheads and the ceiling. As the ship's compartments began to flood, water simply slopped over the top of each bulkhead. There was nothing to stop *Titanic* going down.

When lookout Frederick Fleet saw the iceberg from the crow's nest he called the bridge and struck the warning bell three times: the signal for danger ahead.

Titanic's bulkheads had a series of watertight doors that could be closed from the bridge, or manually. After the collision, some doors were shut and others left open.

LITTLE TIME LEFT

When the *Titanic* collided with the iceberg, some of the passengers and crew felt a bump like the ship "had gone over 1,000 marbles". Captain Smith had also noticed something and was quickly on deck to hear the news. He immediately went down into the engine room with the ship's designer, Thomas Andrews, who was also on board. The men could see water coming through the hull and Andrews calculated *Titanic* had a total of two hours before it sank.

From his bridge, Captain Smith realized two horrifying facts.

1: There were not enough lifeboats on *Titanic* for all of the passengers.

2: As captain, he was expected to go down with the ship.

★ EYEWITNESS ACCOUNT ★

This letter was written by first-class passenger Dr Washington Dodge about the moments after *Titanic's* collision with the iceberg.

> ❝ *Having been told that there was no danger, and believing such to be the fact from the general conduct of the passengers & such officers as I saw I insisted that my family remain in bed and await developments… I asked our steward who was standing there what he had heard — He replied the order has just come down for all passengers to put on life preservers.* ❞

★ **WASHINGTON DODGE**

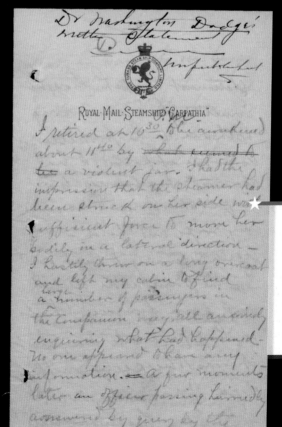

Dodge wrote the letter after being rescued by the *Carpathia*, the boat that picked up *Titanic* survivors from their lifeboats.

WOMEN & CHILDREN FIRST

FORTY-FIVE MINUTES AFTER *Titanic* collided with the iceberg, Captain Edward Smith ordered women and children to be lowered into the lifeboats. The ship's officers carried out the order differently: some allowed men on to the boats and others lowered boats with empty seats.

> *As I was put into the boat, he [Daniel Marvin, her husband] cried to me, 'it's all right, little girl, you go. I will stay.' As our boat shoved off he threw me a kiss and that was the last I saw of him.*
>
> ★ **MRS MARY MARVIN**
> **NEWLY MARRIED PASSENGER**

ESCAPE ROUTES

The order to load the lifeboats caused fear and confusion among *Titanic's* passengers. Many didn't want to board them in the bitter cold; others didn't believe *Titanic* would sink. Meanwhile, some third-class passengers found the gates leading to the upper decks were locked.

This *Titanic* biscuit was taken off the ship in Southampton before she sailed and sold for £3,525 in 2001.

Titanic's 20 lifeboats could only carry 1,178 of the estimated 2,200 people on board. However, the first boat to be lowered only had 28 of its 65 seats filled. Others were also lowered less than half-full.

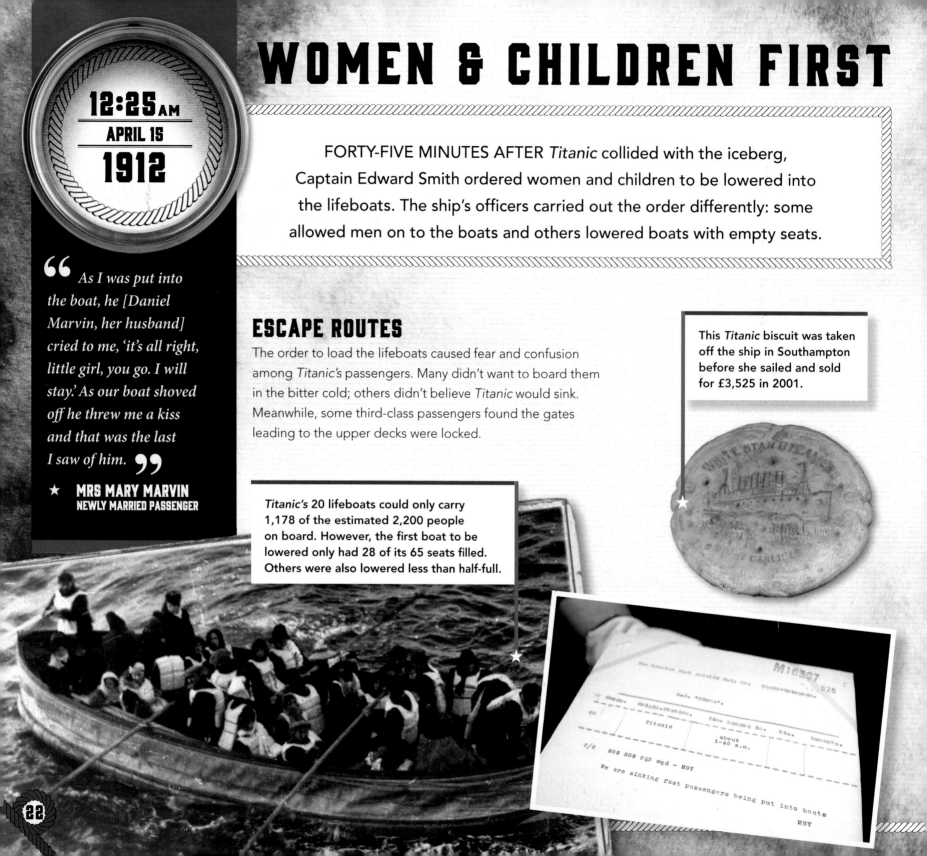

Molly Brown is considered one of the heroes of the *Titanic* disaster who helped raise money for its third-class survivors.

The ship the *Birma* picked up this *Titanic* message: "We have struck iceberg sinking fast come to our assistance."

RADIO DISTRESS SIGNALS

After surveying the damage below decks, Captain Smith immediately ordered radio operator Jack Phillips to send out SOS and CQD (all stations distress) alerts.

> *Come at once. We have struck a berg. It's a CQD, old man… We have struck an iceberg and sinking by the head… We are putting passengers off in small boats. Women and children in boats. Cannot last much longer. Losing power.*

★ **RADIO OPERATOR JACK PHILLIPS**
DISTRESS MESSAGES SENT TO NEARBY SHIPS

M16307

The Russian East Asiatic S.S. Co.   Radio-Telegram   526

S.S. "Birma".

Words.	Origin.Station.	Time handed in.	Via.	Remarks.
	Titanic	11 H.45M.April 14/15 1912.		Distress call Ligs Loud.

Cgd - Sos. from M. G. Y.

We have struck iceberg sinking fast come to our assistance.

Position Lat. 41.46 n.   Lon. 50.14. w.

M.G.Y.

MOLLY BROWN

Margaret Brown was an American millionaire and one of *Titanic's* most famous survivors. She was one of the few people to try to convince rowers on her lifeboat to go back and pick up people from the water. She was known afterwards as 'the unsinkable Molly Brown'.

TIMELINE OF EVENTS

11:40PM
APRIL 14
1912

AFTER *TITANIC* STRUCK THE ICEBERG it took two hours and 40 minutes for her to sink. During this time, *Titanic's* passengers experienced panic, confusion, despair and even quiet acceptance. This timeline describes the pivotal last moments on board the ship.

> *Many brave things were done that night but none more brave than by those few men playing minute after minute as the ship settled quietly lower and lower in the sea.*

★ **LAWRENCE BEESLEY**
TITANIC SURVIVOR DESCRIBING THE SHIP'S ORCHESTRA

IN BOILER ROOM SIX, jets of water gush in after the colliding iceberg makes a thundering crack like a "giant gun going off".

Millionaire John Jacob Astor cut open his lifejacket to show his young wife that it would float.

Lookout Frederick Fleet said he would have spotted the iceberg sooner with binoculars. These had been locked away.

AS FREDERICK FLEET REPORTS THE ICEBERG, *Titanic* is turned hard to the left and its engines are reversed. But it is moving too fast to avoid the tower of ice.

THE SHIP'S STEWARDS begin rousing people from their beds and into lifejackets. Passengers are told to leave their cabins and head for the lifeboats.

TITANIC'S ORCHESTRA IS ORDERED TO PLAY lively ragtime music to keep people calm. Its musicians will go down with the ship. Orchestra leader Wallace Hartley's violin is later sold for £900,000.

Radio operator Jack Phillips kept broadcasting distress signals until *Titanic's* last moments, even though the radio room was flooding.

THIRD-CLASS PASSENGERS had found the stairs leading to the top decks blocked by locked iron gates separating third and first class. When the gates are opened they get lost in the maze of *Titanic's* corridors.

CAPTAIN SMITH ORDERS DISTRESS ROCKETS fired. Around 32km away, Captain Lord of the *Californian* orders no action over the rockets.

WOMEN AND CHILDREN ARE ORDERED into the lifeboats, while men are told to step aside. Water is now flooding into the seamen's cabins at the front of the ship.

ON DECK THERE IS A THUNDEROUS ROAR and hiss as steam escapes from the boilers. The ship's bow has started to tilt downwards.

TITANIC IS NOW CLEARLY SINKING: water reaches the name plate on her bow. Lifeboat number one has been lowered with only 12 people, despite having room for 40 on board.

PANIC SETS IN as passengers realize there are not enough lifeboats. White Star director J. Bruce Ismay jumps aboard collapsible lifeboat C.

OFFICER LOWE FIRES SHOTS to warn people away as lifeboat 14 is lowered. Millionaire Benjamin Guggenheim and his valet change into their best clothes to "go down like gentlemen".

OFFICER LIGHTOLLER AND HIS MEN LOCK ARMS in a circle around collapsible lifeboat D as a crowd surges towards it.

Mr. and Mrs. Isidor Straus

THE LAST LIFEBOAT has been launched. Ida Straus has given up a lifeboat place to stay with millionaire husband Isidor Straus. Passengers left on board become strangely calm.

CAPTAIN SMITH TELLS HIS RADIO OPERATORS AND CREW "now it is every man for himself" and walks alone to his bridge. As *Titanic's* bow takes a nosedive, there is a mass of noise as objects crash forward: plates, pianos and people.

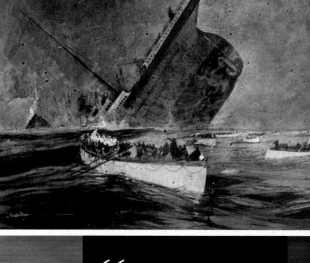

66 *About this time people began jumping from the stern, my friend Milton Long and myself stood beside each other and jumped on the rail. We did not give each other any messages for back home cause neither thought we would ever get back.* 99

★ **JACK B. THAYER**
TITANIC SURVIVOR

AS *TITANIC'S* BOW SINKS LOWER into the water, her stern starts to rise. People move towards the back of the ship. In the first-class smoking room, *Titanic's* designer Thomas Andrews stares into space with his lifejacket lying beside him.

02:18 AM
APRIL 15
1912

THE FINAL MOMENTS

JUST BEFORE 2:20AM, THERE WAS A TERRIBLE ROAR as *Titanic* broke in two. Her stern was pushed back out and rested temporarily on the water's surface. Then she tilted upwards before her final dive down. Passengers holding the back railing prepared for the plunge.

> *Striking the water was like a thousand knives being driven into one's body. The temperature was [-2° Celsius].*
>
> ★ **CHARLES LIGHTOLLER**
> ***TITANIC'S* SECOND OFFICER DESCRIBES JUMPING OFF THE SHIP**

SINKING DOWN

Those left aboard *Titanic* had been worried about being sucked down with the sinking ship. But some survivors reported little suction – those hanging on to the back railing simply stepped off and swam away, as the sea swallowed *Titanic* with a small gulp. Hundreds of passengers thrashed around in the freezing waters trying to stay alive.

Titanic's bow nosedived into the water before the ship broke in two.

LIFEBOAT B

After *Titanic* sank around 30 men swam to collapsible lifeboat B, which lay overturned in the water. Exhausted, some men perched on top of the lifeboat as others died from hypothermia and slipped away. There was little anyone could do to save them.

Officer Lowe put passengers on to other lifeboats and went back to look for survivors, but only got there after most of the screams had died down.

Among the men on collapsible lifeboat B were Archibald Gracie, Jack Thayer and Officer Lightoller.

★ ARCHIBALD GRACIE ★

First-class passenger Colonel Archibald Gracie escaped the sinking *Titanic* by swimming to the overturned collapsible lifeboat B. He was then rescued by the *Carpathia*.

66 *When the ship plunged down I was forced to let go, and I was swirled around and around… Eventually I came to the surface to find the sea a mass of tangled wreckage. Luckily, I was unhurt, and, casting about, managed to seize a wooden grating floating near by.* **99**

★ **COLONEL ARCHIBALD GRACIE**
TITANIC SURVIVOR

RESCUE AND RECOVERY

AFTER THE *TITANIC* SLIPPED BENEATH THE SURFACE, the survivors in lifeboats faced a new ordeal. Around them were the screams of people freezing to death in the water. But within half an hour, there was silence. Now, the long wait for rescue began.

> *There was nothing, just this deathly silence in the dark night with the stars overhead.*
>
> ★ **EVA HART**
> **SEVEN-YEAR-OLD**
> ***TITANIC* SURVIVOR**

Some *Carpathia* passengers took the only known photos of *Titanic* survivors in their lifeboats as they rowed to the ship.

Third-class passenger Frank Goldsmith put his wife and one of his sons aboard a lifeboat, but then went down with the ship. The family are pictured here in 1907.

SURVIVORS

Many *Titanic* survivors were left in shock. Their unsinkable ship was gone and hundreds of the dead were floating in the water nearby. Only one of the lifeboats turned back to help, but it was already too late. Only four people were pulled from the water alive. For those in lifeboats, the temperature was bitterly cold. Many survivors wore only pyjamas and others were soaking wet. Worse still, the wind picked up and the sea became choppy. First-class passengers Molly Brown and the Countess of Rothes took charge of their lifeboats. Others scanned the dark horizon for lights. Then, rockets were seen in the distance: the liner *Carpathia* had arrived.

SAFE AGAIN

The *Carpathia* sailed 93km at full speed through the same ice field that had sunk *Titanic*. As it reached *Titanic's* last given position, *Carpathia* cut its engines and the lifeboats rowed towards her.

Survivors had to climb rope ladders or be pulled up to the *Carpathia* in mail sacks. It took four hours to get everyone on board.

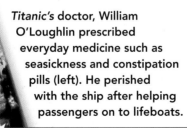

Titanic's doctor, William O'Loughlin prescribed everyday medicine such as seasickness and constipation pills (left). He perished with the ship after helping passengers on to lifeboats.

★ LETTERS OF HORROR ★

Letters recovered from *Titanic* usually praise the ship's luxury and comfort. But those written by survivors aboard the *Carpathia* instead recall the horror of *Titanic's* sinking.

> **❝** *We observed the closing incidents the gradual submergence of the ship forward – The final extinguishment suddenly of all her lights – The final plunge downward... From this time until shortly after 4 in a sea gradually growing rougher with a temperature of extremely cold we rowed about...* **❞**

★ **PASSENGER WASHINGTON DODGE**
LETTER WRITTEN ABOARD THE *CARPATHIA*

SURVIVORS' STORIES

ABOARD *CARPATHIA* SOME FAMILY MEMBERS WERE REUNITED, but many more realized their loved ones were lost. Every one of the 705 survivors had a story to tell. So did the captains of the other ships involved. Heroes and villains soon emerged.

> 66 *After we were picked up on the* Carpathia *my mother came to me, 'cos everytime a lifeboat came I went to see if my father was on it… he wasn't.* 99
>
> ★ **EDITH HAISMAN**
> **15-YEAR-OLD *TITANIC* SURVIVOR**

VILLAIN CAPTAIN

At less than 32km away, the *Californian* was the closest ship to *Titanic* when she sank. Stanley Lord, the *Californian's* captain, had stopped his ship and gone to bed when *Titanic* started firing its distress rockets. Lord's crew woke him with the news, but Lord told them to ignore the rockets. He was painted as a villain for not coming to *Titanic's* rescue.

The survivors' experiences were recorded in letters on the liner *Carpathia* during its voyage to New York.

Captain Rostron (above) was given a silver cup by *Titanic's* survivors in recognition of his heroic service.

HERO CAPTAIN

Carpathia captain Arthur Rostron was considered one of the great heroes of the *Titanic* tragedy. He raced to *Titanic's* rescue without a moment's thought, despite the risk of icebergs in his path. When *Carpathia* arrived its whole crew was on standby with blankets, hot food and coffee for the survivors.

⭐ LAST, LATE APPOINTMENT ⭐

Assistant Surgeon Dr John Edward Simpson was a late appointment to *Titanic's* staff. But his new position was to be his last: Simpson would go down with the ship.

❝ *I have the honour to request that I may be permitted to transfer… to professional duties as Ship's Surgeon in the White Star Line & I am prevented from carrying out all my duties… for some time…* ❞

⭐ **DR JOHN EDWARD SIMPSON**
LETTER REQUESTING A TRANSFER FROM THE ARMY MEDICAL CORPS TO TITANIC

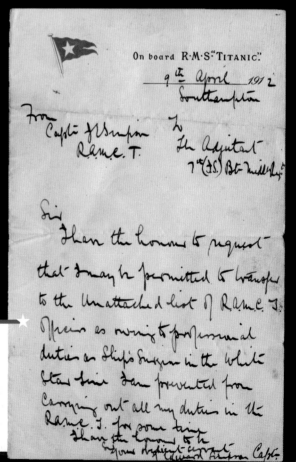

RING

Carl and Selma Asplund agreed to stay together with their five children when *Titanic* began sinking. But only Selma and her children Alex and Lillian survived, after being thrown into a lifeboat. Carl's body was later recovered along with his wedding ring and pocket watch. Lillian died in 2006 at 99 years old. She was one of the three last *Titanic* survivors.

Carl and Selma Asplund's wedding rings were auctioned in 2009, alongside Carl's pocket watch and the family's *Titanic* ticket.

These name plaques from one of *Titanic's* lifeboats were sold at auction in 2006 for £32,000.

Dr Simpson's hurriedly written letter is dated April 9: the day before *Titanic* sailed.

WHAT HAPPENED?

FOR MANY YEARS, IT WAS THOUGHT THE ICEBERG tore massive gashes in *Titanic's* side. But instead, the iceberg probably only popped the rivets out of the hull's steel plates as it scraped past. This opened gaps between the plates where the water could gush in.

Titanic could stay afloat if four of her 16 compartments flooded, but already after 10 minutes, five compartments were taking on water.

As *Titanic* takes on water, she tilts forwards. This causes more water to slop over the watertight bulkheads into further compartments.

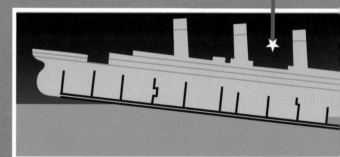

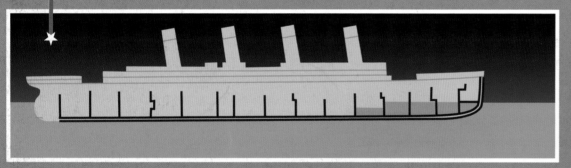

The tremendous pressure of the water on *Titanic's* hull, causes her to break in two.

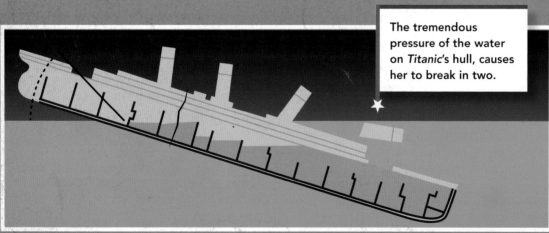

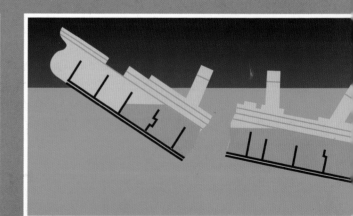

BOILER ROOM DOOR

Titanic had state-of-the-art bulkhead doors that could be closed electronically from the bridge. This would stop water passing from one compartment to the next. However, *Titanic* could only stay afloat if four – not five, as was the case – of its compartments were flooded. Shutting the bulkhead doors, therefore, could only slow and not stop it sinking.

This photo shows the watertight door in boiler room six. The boiler was in *Titanic*'s fifth compartment.

LIFESAVING KEY

Unlike the lifeboats, there were enough lifejackets for every passenger on board *Titanic*. The lifejackets would keep a wearer afloat, but could offer little protection against the freezing seawater.

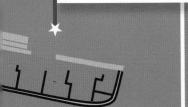

The two parts split, then finally land nearly 600m apart on the seabed.

This locker key to *Titanic*'s lifejackets was one of the objects recovered from the wreck.

> " *Keep out; shut up, I'm working: Cape Race.* "
>
> ★ **TITANIC RADIO OPERATOR JACK PHILLIPS**
> RESPONSE TO THE RADIO OPERATOR OF THE *CALIFORNIAN*,
> WHO WAS SENDING A WARNING OF ICEBERGS IN THE AREA

Jack Phillips (pictured above) was one of *Titanic*'s radio operators. The system used Morse code to send and receive messages.

INQUIRIES AND INTRIGUE

THE NEWS THAT THE UNSINKABLE *TITANIC* HAD GONE DOWN with the loss of over 1,500 lives stunned the world. As the *Carpathia* landed in New York with the survivors, politicians demanded answers about the disaster. A US Senate inquiry into the tragedy began immediately.

> 66 *What do you think I am? Do you believe that I'm the sort that would have left that ship as long as there were any women and children on board?* 99
>
> ★ **J. BRUCE ISMAY,**
> **CHAIRMAN OF THE**
> **WHITE STAR LINE**

INQUIRY ROOM

Senators grilled White Star chairman J. Bruce Ismay when he appeared before the inquiry. Why were there not enough lifeboats on board for every passenger? Did Ismay pressure Captain Smith to make *Titanic* go faster, to break a record? Ismay argued that he had done nothing wrong.

WILLIAM ALDEN SMITH

The US Senator William Alden Smith organized the inquiry into the *Titanic* disaster to begin the day after *Carpathia* arrived in New York. Senators and reporters at the inquiry heard dramatic and sometimes shocking testimony from *Titanic's* survivors. The inquiry found Captain Smith's "indifference to danger" had helped cause the tragedy.

Smith was waiting for *Carpathia* when she landed to tell survivors of their duty to appear before the inquiry.

ISMAY'S CABINS

J. Bruce Ismay had stayed in *Titanic's* lavish B-52 parlour suite and then shut himself away in the doctor's cabin on board *Carpathia*. The world wanted to know why Ismay had boarded a lifeboat when women and children were left aboard *Titanic* to die.

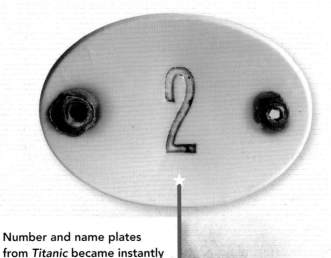

Number and name plates from *Titanic* became instantly popular with trophy hunters.

★ PLANS OF THE SHIP ★

After the US inquiry had finished, survivors had to give evidence again at the UK inquiry. Large plans of *Titanic* were provided to help understand the layout of the ship.

> 66 *The Court, having carefully inquired into the circumstances of the above mentioned shipping casualty [the* Titanic *disaster], finds, for the reasons appearing in the annex hereto, that the loss of the said ship was due to collision with an iceberg, brought about by the excessive speed at which the ship was being navigated.* 99

★ **CONCLUSION OF THE BRITISH INQUIRY INTO WHY *TITANIC* SANK**

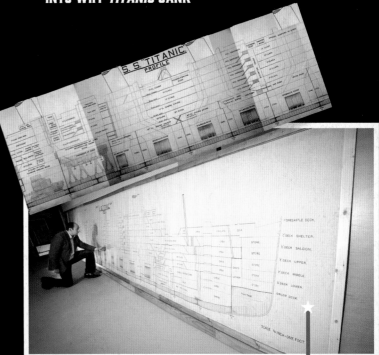

The *Titanic* inquiry plans were found in a rubbish skip in the 1970s and later sold for £220,000.

9:00 AM

MAY 2

1912

" *I thought her unsinkable and I based my opinion on the best expert advice.* "

★ **PHILLIP FRANKLIN**
WHITE STAR LINE
VICE PRESIDENT

SURVIVING CREW AND PASSENGERS had to relive their ordeal at both the US and UK inquiries. The British inquiry lasted 36 days and led to changes in maritime safety that are still in effect today.

ICE PATROL

After the *Titanic* disaster, the US Navy employed two of its cruisers to patrol Iceberg Alley and warn ships in the area of icebergs. Then in 1914, 13 North Atlantic countries created the International Ice Patrol. Today the patrol still searches for icebergs using planes and ships fitted with radar and underwater sonar systems.

An Ice Patrol crew member here scans a chart. Every year the patrol lays a wreath where *Titanic* sank.

These huge icebergs were spotted in 2017 near where *Titanic* sank. Over 450 icebergs had floated into the area within one week.

ARRIVALS

Landing cards such as these were needed by *Titanic* survivors landing in New York aboard the *Carpathia*. This card bears the name Caroline Bonnell, who sailed on *Titanic* with her cousin Mary Natalie Wick and uncle George. George did not survive.

Caroline Bonnell's landing card was part of her scrapbook of *Titanic* memorabilia. Bonnell said she had joked about seeing an iceberg before the ship sailed.

SHIP'S EVIDENCE

Captain Smith used *Titanic's* compass to plot an often-used course across the North Atlantic and through Iceberg Alley. While travelling through ice fields it was not common practice for ships to reduce their speed. For these reasons, the UK *Titanic* inquiry ruled Smith had behaved like any other captain of the time – although it also found *Titanic* was going too fast.

The wood on this *Titanic* compass stand has been eaten away by a type of clam commonly known as shipworm.

★ LIFEBOATS FOR ALL ★

The UK and US inquiries both agreed on one thing: from that point on all ships would have to carry enough lifeboats for every passenger aboard.

> 66 *I feel that the small number of steerage [third class] survivors was thus due to the fact that they got no definite warning before the ship was really doomed, when most of the lifeboats had departed… No general alarm was given, no ship's officers formally assembled, no orderly routine was attempted or organized system of safety begun.* 99

★ **US SENATOR WILLIAM ALDEN SMITH**
EXPLAINING SOME OF THE INQUIRY'S FINDINGS

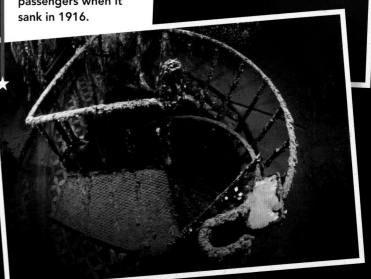

Divers by the wreck of *Titanic's* sister ship *Britannic*, which had enough lifeboats to save most of its passengers when it sank in 1916.

CHAPTER 3

★ **SEARCH FOR THE** ★
SHIPWRECK

1985

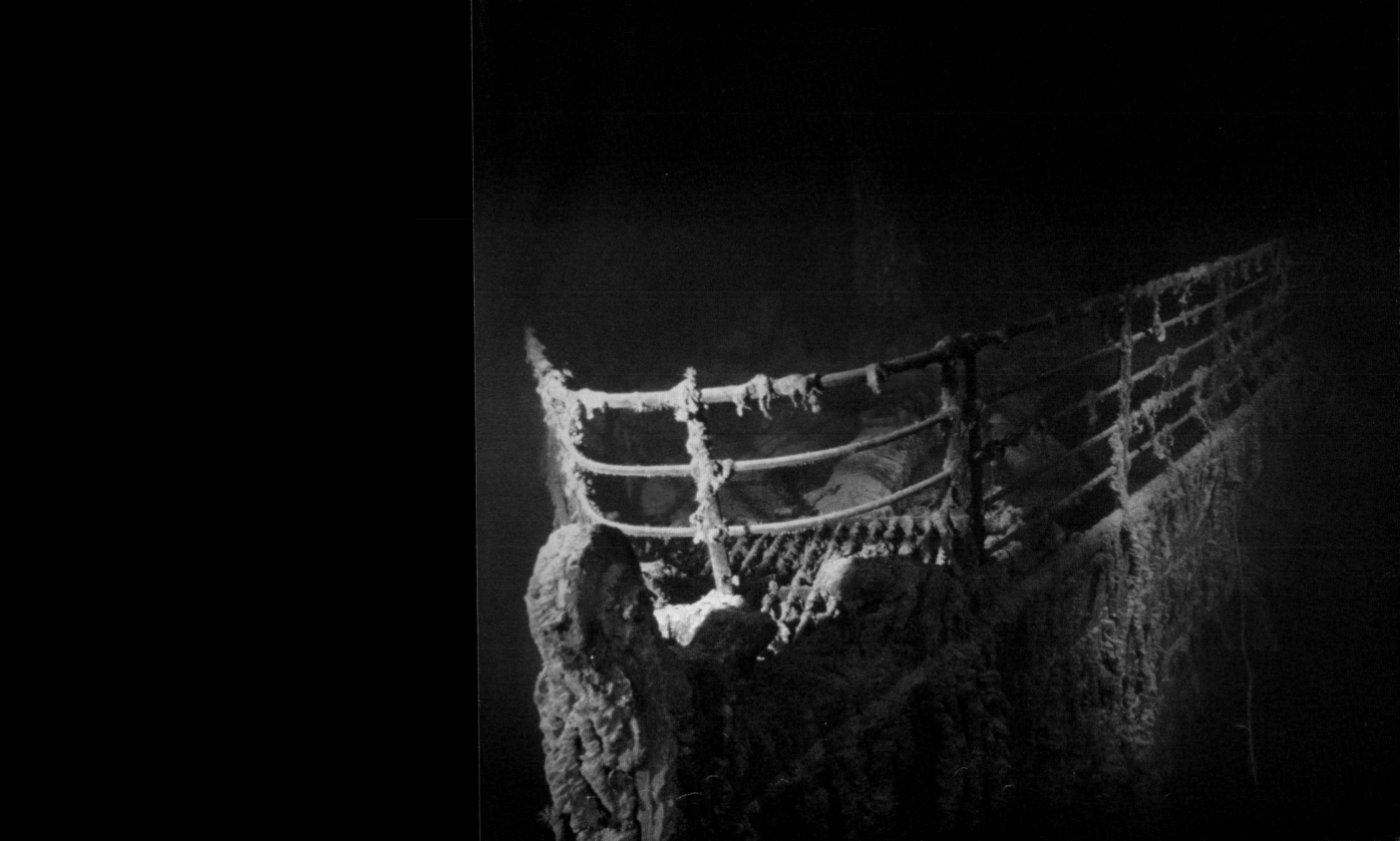

DEEP-SEA EXPLORERS

EXPLORERS BEGAN SEARCHING FOR *TITANIC* IN THE 1970s, but nobody could find her. In 1985, Robert Ballard set out to locate the shipwreck using cameras attached to an underwater craft. Somewhere, about 4km down on the ocean floor was *Titanic*.

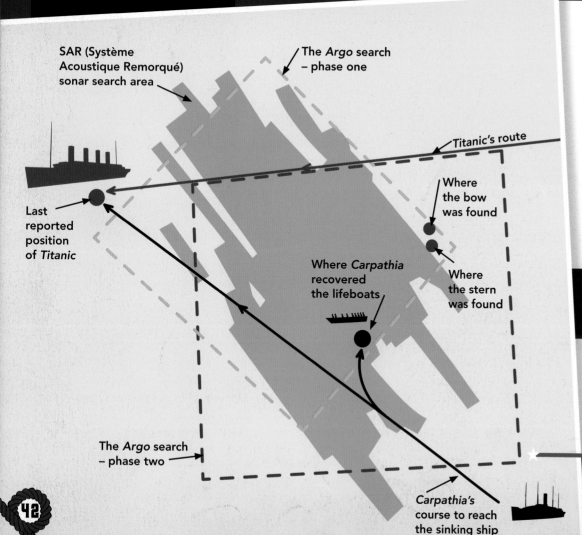

SAR (Système Acoustique Remorqué) sonar search area

The *Argo* search – phase one

Titanic's route

Last reported position of *Titanic*

Where the bow was found

Where *Carpathia* recovered the lifeboats

Where the stern was found

The *Argo* search – phase two

Carpathia's course to reach the sinking ship

X MARKS THE SPOT

Explorers looked for *Titanic* based on the distress coordinates sent by the ship's radio operator on the night she sank. When the wreck was not found in this location, searchers began large 'sweeps' of the ocean floor around it.

This map shows the rectangular search area explored by *Titanic* expeditions in the 1980s. Up until 1985, there was no sign of the shipwreck.

TREASURE HUNT

Ballard's *Titanic* expedition began with a top secret mission for the US Navy. If Ballard located two missing submarine wrecks, then he could use the Navy's equipment to search for *Titanic*. Ballard found the submarines, but then only had 12 days to search for *Titanic*. His team quickly began broad sweeps over the area where *Titanic* might have sunk. But after seven days, nothing had been found.

Argo **was a deep-sea vehicle, equipped with sonar, cameras and lights, that could make sweeps of the ocean floor.**

Robert Ballard was a marine geologist and naval oceograph who had dreamed of finding the wreck of *Titanic* from childhoc He led his first *Titanic* expedition in 1977.

❝ *I'd only have 12 days to do what others had not done in 60. That's all that was left. We had to do our mission for the Navy first and naval officers aboard would then approve it when we finished their mission and were now free to pursue the* Titanic. ❞

★ **ROBERT BALLARD**
TITANIC **EXPEDITION LEADER**

Ballard became an instant celebrity after finding *Titanic* and everybody wanted to interview him. Here, he discusses the discovery at a news conference.

SPOTTING THE SHIP

1:05 AM
SEPTEMBER 1
1985

IN THE EARLY HOURS OF SEPTEMBER 1, 1985, the explorers looking for *Titanic* were ready to give up their search. On board research vessel the *Knorr,* the only thing the crew could see through the video monitors linked to *Argo* was the murky ocean bottom. Then, through the gloom, a large ship's boiler came into view. *Titanic* had been found!

❝ *The first reaction was celebration, we all jumped up shouting because we were near the end of the expedition and we thought we were going to fail. But that was followed quickly by a realization of where we were... we started seeing where the bodies had landed: this was a cemetery.* ❞

★ **ROBERT BALLARD**
TITANIC EXPEDITION LEADER

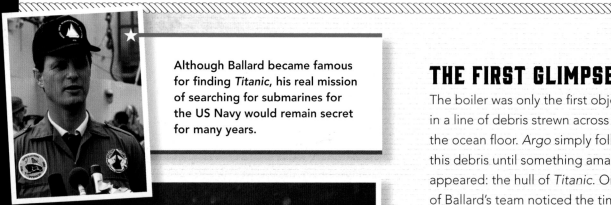

★ Although Ballard became famous for finding *Titanic*, his real mission of searching for submarines for the US Navy would remain secret for many years.

THE FIRST GLIMPSE

The boiler was only the first object in a line of debris strewn across the ocean floor. *Argo* simply followed this debris until something amazing appeared: the hull of *Titanic*. One of Ballard's team noticed the time was just after 1am. Not long after that time 73 years ago, *Titanic* had gone down at 2:20am, taking with it the lives of over 1,500 men, women and children. This made the discovery a particularly strange, eerie moment for the crew aboard the *Knorr*.

★ Twenty-nine boilers were fed by 159 coal furnaces to power *Titanic*'s two enormous steam engines.

44

TITANIC SPECIFICATIONS

WIDTH:
28m

TOP SPEED:
23 knots

LENGTH:
269m

CAPACITY:
3,547 passengers and crew

FORGOTTEN FOOTPRINT

Metal ship parts were not the only objects found in the debris field around *Titanic*. There were also reminders of the human cost of the tragedy, including personal items belonging to the passengers and crew. One upsetting sight was two shoes together, still laced. This showed where a person had fallen on the sea floor, their body long since decayed.

PROPELLER POWER

Among the *Titanic* objects littering the sea floor was one of the massive propellers that powered her through the water. On her maiden voyage across the Atlantic, *Titanic* had set out to impress. White Star director J. Bruce Ismay had wanted *Titanic* to reach New York in record time. However, the British inquiry had found *Titanic* had been travelling too fast through the ice field on the night she sank. The propeller had been snapped from the hull as *Titanic* went down.

Here, *Titanic's* shipbuilders gaze up at its massive propellers: a marvel of modern engineering.

The absence of light and air on the seabed means it takes longer for objects like leather shoes to decay.

45

TITANIC FOUND!

THERE COULD BE NO MISTAKING *TITANIC'S* MASSIVE MACHINERY strewn across the sea floor. For 73 years, the ship's boilers, propellers and cranes had lain undisturbed two and a half miles below the surface. Now, the lights aboard *Argo* lit up the world's most famous shipwreck.

> *Sure enough I saw the image of a big ship's boiler – Titanic's. I didn't yelp or shout. In fact for a few seconds I didn't say anything.*
>
> ★ **ROBERT BALLARD**
> ***TITANIC* EXPEDITION LEADER**

LIFTING THE LID

Seeing *Titanic's* hull was both a thrill and a shock for the crew of the *Knorr*. Odd, brown icicle-shaped bacteria covered the metal hull and its machinery. Ballard called these bacteria shapes "rusticles." Rusticles covered one of *Titanic's* cargo cranes, which was still attached to the ship.

ONE GOOD TURN

Embedded in the sea floor was *Titanic's* massive starboard propeller. The largest two of *Titanic's* three propellers sat on the starboard and port sides. These had three blades, weighed 39 tonnes and were 7m in diameter. The bronze propellers had not been corroded by the seawater.

Titanic was fitted with eight cargo cranes to lift cargo and baggage from its hold.

Titanic was originally called 'SS' *Titanic*, which stands for 'Screw Steamer'. This was because it was driven by propellers, also called screws.

OFF THE BOIL

Titanic's boilers had been among the largest ever built for a seagoing vessel. When Ballard saw such a boiler resting on the sea bottom he felt sure the shipwreck had been found.

Titanic's 29 boilers are here pictured in 1912 before they were transported to the ship to be fitted.

After the boiler broke away from the sinking ship it landed on its side.

Ballard and his crew members Jean-Louis Michel and Jean Jerry are pictured in front of the *Argo* submersible. The expedition had been a partnership between French and American oceanographers.

❝ *The* Titanic *lies in 13,000 feet of water on a gently sloping alpine-like countryside overlooking a small canyon below… There is no light at this great depth and little can be found. It is a quiet and peaceful and fitting place for the remains of this greatest of sea tragedies to rest. May it remain that way and may God bless those found souls.* ❞

★ **ROBERT BALLARD**
TITANIC EXPEDITION LEADER

UNDERWATER TOMB

SEEING *TITANIC'S* BOILER ON THE SEA FLOOR was a great moment of triumph and celebration for Ballard's team. But the mood soon changed. Among the wreckage lay items belonging to people, including bags and hats. This was not just a shipwreck: it was a graveyard.

> *I could see the Titanic as she slipped nose first into the glassy water. Around me were the ghostly shapes of the lifeboats and the piercing shouts and screams of people freezing to death in the water.*

★ **ROBERT BALLARD
TALKS ABOUT DISCOVERING
THE *TITANIC* WRECK**

These battered cooking pots made of copper, zinc and brass have withstood the corrosion usually caused by seawater and time.

EVERYDAY ITEMS

Kitchen cooking pots were among the items in the vast debris field littering the sea floor around the wreck. *Titanic* had 62 kitchen staff, including chefs, cooks, bakers and butchers. These people were responsible for cooking over 6,000 meals every day for the ship's passengers. However, only 13 of *Titanic's* kitchen staff survived the disaster.

PERIOD CLOTHING

Top hats were an essential part of formal evening wear for first class passengers aboard *Titanic*. They would normally have been worn with black tailcoat jacket and trousers, a white waistcoat and a bow tie. Some wearers of these 1912-style tuxedos also walked with a cane, which was considered highly fashionable.

CLOSE SHAVE

Only third-class passengers needed their own shaving kits for the trip. First- and second-class passengers could be shaved by one of *Titanic's* three barbers. Of these, only the chief barber, Augustus Weikman, survived the disaster. Weikman was thrown into the water as *Titanic* began sinking and stayed afloat by clinging on to wreckage. Amazingly, Weikman was tossed towards a lifeboat on a wave caused by an exploding boiler. He was then hauled aboard.

TREASURE STASH

This leather bag discovered in the *Titanic* wreck contained a rare hoard of expensive jewellery. During *Titanic's* final moments, bags were stuffed with jewellery and money from the ship's safes.

HISTORIC TOILETRIES

This pomade recovered from the *Titanic* wreck was made by London company H.P. Truefitt, which sold men's scented hair and toiletry products. Pomade would have been a popular product at the two barber shops aboard *Titanic*. Neatly trimmed moustaches and hair slicked back with pomade were fashionable among wealthy men in the early 1900s.

FROZEN IN TIME

> *We hadn't dreamed people would get so excited about our finding the ship.*
>
> ★ **ROBERT BALLARD**
> ON THE MEDIA RESPONSE TO DISCOVERING *TITANIC*

WITH *TITANIC* FOUND, the shipwreck could be explored using the *Argo* submersible. With its cameras and lights, *Argo* quickly cleared up some of *Titanic's* enduring mysteries.

Pieces of the hull had been torn away from *Titanic* as it broke in two on its way to the bottom.

NEW EVIDENCE

As *Titanic* sank, some of those aboard the lifeboats reported that the ship had broken in two. Others said it went down in one piece. Using *Argo*, Ballard showed the ship's hull had broken into two pieces. These now lay nearly 600m apart on the ocean floor.

BREAKING NEWS

The discovery of *Titanic* on September 1, 1985, grabbed headlines around the world. Ballard immediately began giving interviews to eager reporters via his ship's radio. Then, only three days after the find, news helicopters flew to Ballard's ship to collect the first underwater photos of *Titanic*. Everyone wanted a glimpse of the wreck. This was a taste of the media storm awaiting Ballard when he returned to shore.

The New York Times was the first newspaper to report *Titanic* was sinking when others claimed everyone had been rescued. It would report the ship's discovery 73 years later.

The New York Times.

"All the News That's Fit to Print."

THE WEATHER.

NEW YORK, TUESDAY, APRIL 16, 1912.—TWENTY-FOUR PAGES.

ONE CENT

TITANIC SINKS FOUR HOURS AFTER HITTING ICEBERG; 866 RESCUED BY CARPATHIA, PROBABLY 1250 PERISH; ISMAY SAFE, MRS. ASTOR MAYBE, NOTED NAMES MISSING

The Lost Titanic Being Towed Out of Belfast Harbor.

PARTIAL LIST OF THE SAVED.

CAPT. E. J. SMITH, Commander of the Titanic.

Ballard's plaque reads: "In memory of those souls who perished with the 'Titanic' April 14th/15th 1912."

COMMEMORATIVE PLAQUE

Although Ballard was against taking objects from *Titanic*, he was the first to leave a plaque on the ship honouring the dead. Over the years many similar plaques have been placed where the ship's bridge once lay. Some people have criticized these plaques, saying it is no different from leaving litter on the wreck.

RECOVERING OBJECTS

AFTER HE DISCOVERED *TITANIC*, ROBERT BALLARD PROMISED never to take anything from the wreck. To him, the ship's final resting place should remain undisturbed in respect for the dead. But in 1987, a new expedition to retrieve objects from *Titanic* began.

> " *To bring up those things from a mass sea grave just to make a few thousand pounds shows a dreadful insensitivity and greed.* "
>
> ★ **EVA HART**
> *TITANIC* SURVIVOR

The bowl is engraved with the words: 'RMS Titanic Maiden Voyage 1912' and '1st Class Barbershop 401'.

SHIP SALES

The 1987 *Titanic* expedition was organized to recover objects from the wreck and put them up for sale. Many people would pay big money to own a piece of the *Titanic* story. This souvenir bowl (right) was purchased from *Titanic's* first class barbershop. After being recovered from the shipwreck, the bowl was sold at auction for £1,560. During the 1987 expedition, 1,800 objects were brought ashore. More than 5,500 objects have been retrieved over the years.

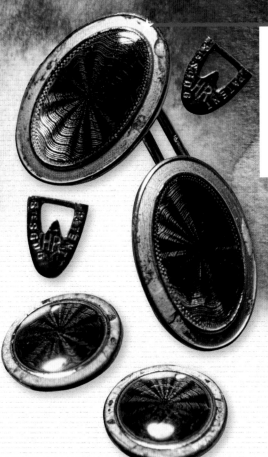

These men's cufflinks and studs, made of gold and green enamel, show off the wealth of *Titanic*'s first-class passengers.

MYSTERY

This diamond ring, alongside gold cufflinks and a gold ribbon broach with diamonds, were inside the leather bag discovered on *Titanic*. The owner of the jewellery is unknown.

MUSEUM PIECES

Not every object recovered from *Titanic* has been put up for sale. Some, such as these cufflinks (above) and ring (right), made up part of an exhibition called 'Jewels of the Titanic'. The cufflinks and ring were found inside a leather bag that was entrusted to the ship's purser, the person responsible for valuables on *Titanic*. Many first-class maids were trying to collect their mistresses' valuables from the purser when *Titanic* began to sink.

The high-end 18-karat gold-and-platinum ring is encrusted with 60 diamonds.

FORGOTTEN DIARIES AND LETTERS

Diaries and letters were among the everyday objects recovered from the *Titanic* wreck. Found inside chests and cupboards, these paper items had miraculously survived the saltwater.

> *It was a brilliant crowd. Jewels flashed from the gowns of the women. And, oh, the dear women, how fondly they wore their latest Parisian gown! It was the first time that most of them had an opportunity to display their newly acquired finery.*

★ **JACQUES FUTRELLE**
FIRST-CLASS PASSENGER IN A LETTER

This diary kept by an unknown *Titanic* passenger features a pressed flower between its pages.

"TITANIC" MEMORIAL.
ERECTED TO THE IMPERISHABLE MEMORY
OF THOSE GALLANT BELFAST MEN WHOSE
NAMES ARE HERE INSCRIBED AND WHO
LOST THEIR LIVES ON THE 15ᵗʰ APRIL 1912

THOMAS ANDREWS JUN.
WILLIAM HENRY MARSH PARR
FREDERICK CHISHOLM

8:00PM
NOVEMBER 1
1997

> ❝ *My primary motivation was to go dive the Mount Everest of shipwrecks.* ❞
>
> ★ **JAMES CAMERON**
> **ON MAKING THE 1997 BLOCKBUSTER *TITANIC***

FASCINATION WITH THE *TITANIC* DISASTER began with the news of her sinking. Only 29 days later the first film was released. It starred an actual *Titanic* survivor. More films followed, until director James Cameron topped them all with his 1997 film, *Titanic*.

Cameron is photographed alongside the 12-tonne, lime green *Deepsea Challenger*.

DEEPSEA CHALLENGER

To shoot footage for his *Titanic* film, director James Cameron organized an expedition to the wreck itself. He filmed the ship from the *Deepsea Challenger* submarine, fitted with special lights and cameras.

TITANIC THE FILM

The 1997 film *Titanic* won 11 Academy Awards, made over $2 billion, and is one of the most successful films of all time. Director James Cameron built a 90% scale model of *Titanic* to film the sinking and made his star Kate Winslet ill by keeping her in the water for too long.

A *Mir* submarine films *Titanic* for the *Ghosts of the Abyss* documentary.

Titanic the film featured a love-story between characters played by Kate Winslet and Leonardo DiCaprio.

Cameron's replica *Titanic* could be lifted on a giant hinge.

James Cameron directs his stars in freezing seawater. Kate Winslet caught pneumonia as a result.

GHOSTS OF THE ABYSS

After releasing *Titanic*, James Cameron returned to the shipwreck to film a documentary about the disaster. Using two remote-controlled submarines, Cameron was able to reach and film parts of *Titanic's* interior not seen in 91 years. Cameron then showed computer-generated images of how *Titanic* originally looked alongside those of the wreck. He also filmed several reenactments of the events that took place the night *Titanic* sank.

Titanic's interior is lit by underwater lights for *Ghosts of the Abyss.*

THE NEVER-ENDING STORY

ALTHOUGH *TITANIC* HAS LAIN ON THE SEA FLOOR for over 100 years, she is more famous today than ever before. Countless films, TV shows, books, songs, musicals and games have been made about the disaster. Everyone has heard of *Titanic*.

MEMORABILIA

This snow globe of *Titanic* sinking shows how much the disaster is part of modern popular culture. There are many different *Titanic* toys around today, including model ships for the bath that sink slowly and then break in half.

This is only one of dozens of *Titanic* snow globes on offer. Others include rotating musical *Titanic* snow globes that sit on top of their own grand staircase.

The Spirit Of TITANIC

DOLLED UP

Titanic dolls have been big business for many years. Today's dolls are most commonly of Kate Winslet and Leonardo DiCaprio, who starred in the film *Titanic*. But porcelain dolls also lie among the objects left around the *Titanic* wreck. A head belonging to such a doll was filmed by Robert Ballard during his 1986 expedition. It gave Ballard's crew a fright when they saw it staring at them.

This cloth rag-doll is of one of the maids who served aboard *Titanic*.

TITANIC BOOKS

There are over 600 books about *Titanic* written in English alone. The first books were accounts by survivors published in 1912. One of the most famous is by Colonel Archibald Gracie, who escaped *Titanic* by jumping off the ship as it sank (see page 29).

Many new books on the *Titanic* disaster are still written and published every year.

A NIGHT TO REMEMBER

Walter Lord's 1955 *A Night to Remember* is a non-fiction book based on interviews with over 60 *Titanic* survivors. The book was a huge success and was later adapted for theatre, TV and film. Lord gained his lifelong fascination with *Titanic* after travelling aboard its sister ship, *Olympic*, as a boy. He later worked as a consultant on the 1997 film *Titanic*.

Walter Lord followed up *A Night to Remember* (right) with his 1986 *Titanic* title *The Night Lives On*.

★ DOROTHY GIBSON ★

Dorothy Gibson was an actress who survived the *Titanic* disaster and then starred in the first *Titanic* movie, *Saved from the Titanic*, released only a month after it sank.

> ❝ *As I started to walk across the boat I noticed how lopsided the deck was... I will never forget the terrible cry that rang out from people who were thrown into the sea and others who were afraid for their loved ones.* ❞

★ **DOROTHY GIBSON**
***TITANIC* SURVIVOR AND ACTRESS DESCRIBING THE SINKING**

Gibson appeared in *Saved from the Titanic* wearing the same clothes she had escaped the ship in.

RUSTICLES AND DECAY

OVER A CENTURY SINCE SHE SANK, *Titanic* continues to fascinate and surprise people. However, years of sitting on the ocean floor have taken their toll. Rust and decay have worn away the ship and one day there will be nothing left.

> *The deep sea is the largest museum on our planet, but there's no lock on its door.*
> ★ **ROBERT BALLARD**

SHIP DESTRUCTION

Today, reddish brown bacteria called rusticles cover the *Titanic* wreck. Experts say by 2030 rusticles will have eaten away the ship, leaving only a stain on the sea floor. To preserve the wreck, Robert Ballard has suggested spraying it with special anti-corrosive paint. This will slow down the process of decay.

This top of one of *Titanic's* 9m high engines will one day rust into nothing.

CLASS-WARE

Recovered objects such as this glassware have either been sold at auction or put on display at *Titanic* exhibitions. Taking objects from *Titanic* remains controversial. Families of the survivors say the wreck is a gravesite and should be left alone. Others argue that *Titanic's* objects are important archeological artifacts that should be shared. Some simply want to make money from the disaster.

This glassware from *Titanic's* first-class dining saloon is a reminder of the class divisions aboard the ship.

BREAK DOWN

Everyday objects recovered from *Titanic* such as this toast rack and bottle holder (below) tell a story of life aboard the ship. The fuzzy green coating on the objects also shows the process of corrosion that attacks bronze and copper items submerged in saltwater. If left undisturbed and untreated, *Titanic* objects such as these will eventually dissolve away. Many say this is why its objects should be recovered.

Sidney Sedunary's pocket watch is part of a permanent *Titanic* exhibition at Southampton's Seacity museum.

The first-class bottle holder and toast rack were used to hold wine and toast alongside silver bowls of caviar.

TIME OF DEATH

This watch was recovered from the body of *Titanic* steward Sidney Sedunary. It stopped at 1:50am, 30 minutes before the unsinkable *Titanic* was lost. It is an eerie reminder of the 1,500 people who were lost with her.

INDEX

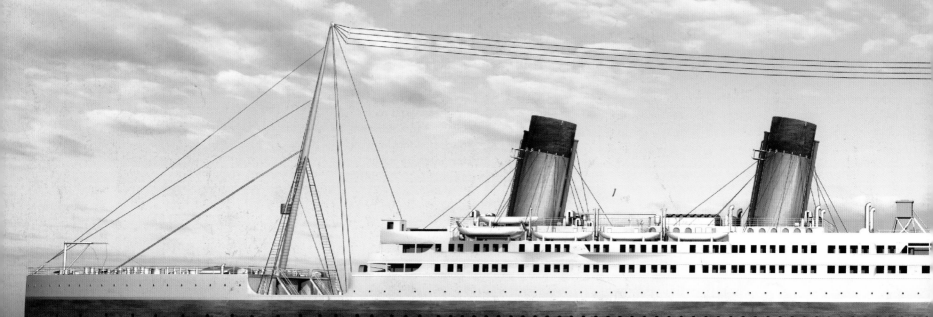

PICTURE CREDITS

The publishers would like to thank the following sources for their kind permission to reproduce the pictures in this book.

Page 4 Emory Kristof/National Geographic/Getty Images, 5 Bob Thomas/Popperfoto/Getty Images, 7 (top) Phil Yeomans/REX/Shutterstock, (right) Granger Historical Picture Archive/Alamy Stock Photo, 8 Louisa Gouliamaki/AFP/Getty Images, 8-9 New York Public Library/Science Photo Library, 9 (top & bottom) Patrick Landmann/Science Photo Library, (right) Popperfoto/Getty Images, 11 (top) Zuma Press Inc./Alamy Stock Photo, (right) Onslow Auctions Limited/Mary Evans Picture Library, (bottom right) Private Collection, 12 (left) Frank Mullen/WireImage, (right) Private Collection, 13 (top) Alain Benainous/Gamma-Rapho via Getty Images, (bottom) Patrick Landmann/Science Photo Library, (right) A.Aldridge/Bournemouth News/REX/Shutterstock, 14 (left) Nils Jorgensen/REX/Shutterstock, (right) Ralph White/CORBIS/Corbis via Getty Images, 15 (top) Corbis Documentary/Getty Images, (right, bottom left, bottom centre) Patrick Landmann/Science Photo Library, (bottom right) PMG/SIPA/REX/Shutterstock, 16 (left) Maniel Dunand/AFP/Getty Images, (right) Universal Images Group/Getty Images, 17 (top & centre) Universal Images Group/Getty Images, (bottom) PA Photos/Topfoto, (right) Les Wilson/REX/Shutterstock, 20 (left) Glenn Copus/Evening Standard /REX/Shutterstock, (right) Public Domain, 21 (left) Mario Tama/Getty Images, (right) The Gilder Lehrman Institute of American History, 22 (left) Public Domain, (bottom right) Topfoto.co.uk, (centre right) REX/Shutterstock, 23 (left) Granger/REX/Shutterstock, (right) Print Collector/Getty Images, 24 (left) Library of Congress, (right) Granger/REX/Shutterstock, (top) Morten Watkins/Solent News/REX/Shutterstock, 25 (top right) Universal History Archive/Universal Images Group/REX/Shutterstock, (centre left) Bournemouth News/REX/Shutterstock, (bottom left) Bettmann/Getty Images, (bottom right) Granger/REX/Shutterstock, 26 (top left) Chronicle/Alamy Stock Photo, (bottom left) Granger Historical Picture Archive/Alamy Stock Photo, (top right) Bob Thomas/Popperfoto/Getty Images, (bottom right) Granger/REX/Shutterstock, 27 (top left) Bettmann/Getty Images, (top centre) ullstein bild/ullstein bild via Getty Images, (top right) Carl Simon/United Archives/UIG via Getty Images, (bottom) Willy Stöwer/ullstein bild via Getty Images, 28 (top) Hulton Archive/Getty Images, (centre) Granger/REX/Shutterstock, (top right) Private Collection, (bottom right) Illustrated London News Ltd/Mary Evans, 31 (top & bottom) & 32 (centre) Library of Congress, (bottom left) Patrick Landmann/Science Photo Library, (centre right) Stephen Barnes/Northern Ireland/Alamy Stock Photo, (right & bottom right) Patrick Landmann/Science Photo Library, 32 (left) Bournemouth News/REX/Shutterstock, (right) DeAgostini/Getty Images, 33 (top) Phil Yeomans/REX/Shutterstock, (bottom) Spencer Platt/Getty Images, (right) HAldridge/Bournemouth News/REX/Shutterstock, 35 (top) United Archives GmbH/Alamy Stock Photo, (bottom centre) H.Aldridge/Bournemouth News/REX/Shutterstock, (centre) Universal Images Group/Getty Images, (right) Pictorial Press Ltd/Alamy Stock Photo, 36 Stock Montage/Getty Images, 37 (top) Granger/REX/Shutterstock, (bottom) Patrick Landmann/Science Photo Library, (right) Private Collection, (bottom right) Bournemouth News/REX/Shutterstock, 38 (left) AP/REX/Shutterstock, (right) Stephan Savoia/AP/REX/Shutterstock, 39 (top left) Mark Sagliocco/Getty Images, (bottom) Patrick Landmann/Science Photo Library, (centre right & bottom right) ITV/REX/Shutterstoc, 40-41 National Geographic Magazines/Getty Images, 42-43 Emory Kristof/National Geographic/Getty Images, 43 (right) Cynthia Johnson/The LIFE Images Collection/Getty Images, 44 & 45 (top) Ralph White/Getty Images, 45 (centre) John Parrot/Stocktrek/Getty Images, (bottom centre) Ralph White/Getty Images, (bottom right) Roslan Rahman/AFP/Getty Images, 46 (centre & bottom) Emory Kristof/National Geographic/Getty Images, 47 (centre) SSPL/Getty Images, (bottom) Ralph White/Getty Images, (right) Sipa Press/REX/Shutterstock, 48 Emory Kristof/National Geographic/Getty Images, 49 (top) Patrick Landmann/Science Photo Library, (centre) Frank Mullen/WireImage/Getty Images, (bottom) Tony Kyriacou/REX/Shutterstock, (right) Mary Altaffer/AP/REX/Shutterstock, 50 (top) Library of Congress, (bottom) Emory Kristof/National Geographic/Getty Images, 51 (left) Granger Historical Picture Archive/Alamy Stock Photo, (right) Emory Kristof/National Geographic/Getty Images, 52 Nils Jorgensen/REX/Shutterstock, 53 (top) Patrick Landmann/Science Photo Library, (bottom) Johnny Clark/AP/REX/Shutterstock, (bottom right) Patrick Landmann/Science Photo Library, 54 Radharc Images/Alamy Stock Photo, 55 VanderWolf Images/Shutterstock, 56 Jason LaVeris/FilmMagic/Getty Images, 57 (top) Earthship Prods./Kobal/REX/Shutterstock, (left) 20th Century Fox/Paramount/Kobal/REX/Shutterstock, (centre) Merie W. Wallace/20th Century Fox/Paramount/Kobal/REX/Shutterstock, (right) Earthship Prods./Kobal/REX/Shutterstock, (bottom left) 20th Century Fox/Paramount/Kobal/REX/Shutterstock, (bottom right) Earthship Prods./Kobal/REX/Shutterstock, 58 (left) DEA/A. Dagli Orti/De Agostini/Getty Images, (right) Richard Gardner/REX/Shutterstock, 59 (top) Stephen Barnes/Northern Ireland/Alamy Stock Photo, (top centre) Marvin Joseph/The Washington Post/Getty Images, (centre) ITV/REX/Shutterstock, (bottom centre) Universal History Archive/REX/Shutterstock, (right) Public Domain, 60 Emory Kristof/National Geographic/Getty Images, 61 (top & bottom) Patrick Landmann/Science Photo Library, (right) Matt Cardy/Getty Images.

Every effort has been made to acknowledge correctly and contact the source and/or copyright holder of each picture and Carlton Books Limited apologises for any unintentional errors or omissions, which will be corrected in future editions of this book.